SO NUTZEN SIE DIESES THEMENHEFT

Sechs Themengebiete führen in die Landeskunde Australiens ein: Das erste, „Welcome", führt zur ersten Orientierung auf der Australienkarte. Hinzu kommen weitere fünf Themengebiete: *History, Way of Life, Lifestyle, Places* und *Wildlife*. Zu jedem der sechs Themengebiete gehören fünf Stationen, die jeweils den vier klassischen Lernbereichen Textarbeit *(Reading)*, Wortschatzarbeit *(Vocabulary)*, Grammatik *(Grammar)* und Textproduktion *(Speaking and Writing)* zugeordnet sind. Als fünfte Station ist für jeden Themenbereich jeweils eine Computerstation vorgesehen, an der Schlüsselfertigkeiten der Internetrecherche geübt werden.

Daraus ergibt sich folgende Matrix, die es erlaubt, einzelne *Skills* oder inhaltliche Themengebiete gesondert herauszugreifen:

	A Reading	B Vocabulary	C Grammar	D Textproduction	E Internet Skills
1. Welcome	Australia – Down under! [Text]	Weather words [Mindmap]	Where to go in Australia [Articles]	Off to Australia [Speaking game]	[Using online dictionaries] included in Station 1B
2. History	Australia Day [Text]	Exploring words [Categorising]	History blockbusters [Active/passive]	Australian legend [Translation]	Search Australia [Choosing keywords]
3. Way of Life	Aboriginal Australia [Text]	In the news [Word jumble]	School of the air [S-Genitive/ plural s]	Life on a sheep station [Conducting an interview]	[Making an Internet research] included in Station 3A
4. Lifestyle	G'day Australia [Text]	Speak Strine! [Matching game]	Christmas in the summer season [Quantifiers]	Beach safety [Interpreting warning signs]	Waltzing Matilda [Using a search engine]
5. Places	In the outback [Text]	Outback-survival words [Picture clues]	Emergency in the outback [Reported speech]	Rescued by the flying doctor service [Writing a news report]	Sightseeing in Sydney [Skimming for information]
6. Wildlife	Deadly creatures [Text]	Animal words [Trimino]	Animal trumps [Comparatives and superlatives]	Who's afraid of spiders? [Writing a story with picture clues]	The Great Barrier Reef [Using an online encyclopaedia]

Bei der Konzeption der Stationen wurde Wert darauf gelegt, dass landeskundliches Wissen eher in den klassischen Stationen vermittelt wird, während die Internetstationen auf eine Erweiterung der „internet literacy" zum Thema Australien abzielen. Sollte die medientechnische Ausstattung an den Schulen ein Hindernis darstellen, können die betreffenden Stationen auch problemlos von der Lehrkraft gestrichen werden. Selbstverständlich eignen sich die Arbeitsblätter aber auch für die selbstständige Arbeit am häuslichen Computer. Im Einzelnen sollen an den Computerstationen der Umgang mit Online-Wörterbüchern und -Enzyklopädien trainiert und die Wahl von Suchbegriffen geübt werden. Es ist eine Station zum *Skimreading* vorgesehen und schließlich soll auch Gelegenheit zu einer komplexeren Internetrecherche gegeben sein.

Die Stationen berücksichtigen die unterschiedlichen Lerntypen, lassen unterschiedliche Sozialformen (Einzel-, Partner- und Gruppenarbeit) zu und erfordern eine Variation der Arbeitsformen.

Es empfiehlt sich, die Arbeitsblätter der Stationen, die zu einem Bereich gehören *(Welcome, History, Way of Life, Lifestyle, Places, Wildlife)*, jeweils auf gleichfarbiges Papier zu kopieren. Die Schülerinnen und Schüler können sich innerhalb der Stationen dann besser orientieren.

Die Attraktivität, Haltbarkeit und Wiederverwendbarkeit der Materialien (Spielkarten, Spielpläne etc.) erhöht sich beträchtlich, wenn sie auf farbigen Karton kopiert und laminiert werden.

Lösungsblätter sollten jeweils getrennt von den Stationen aufbewahrt werden – entweder in einem Ordner bei der Lehrkraft und/oder separat an der Klassenzimmerwand.

MATERIALIEN UND HINWEISE ZU DEN STATIONEN

MAP OF AUSTRALIA

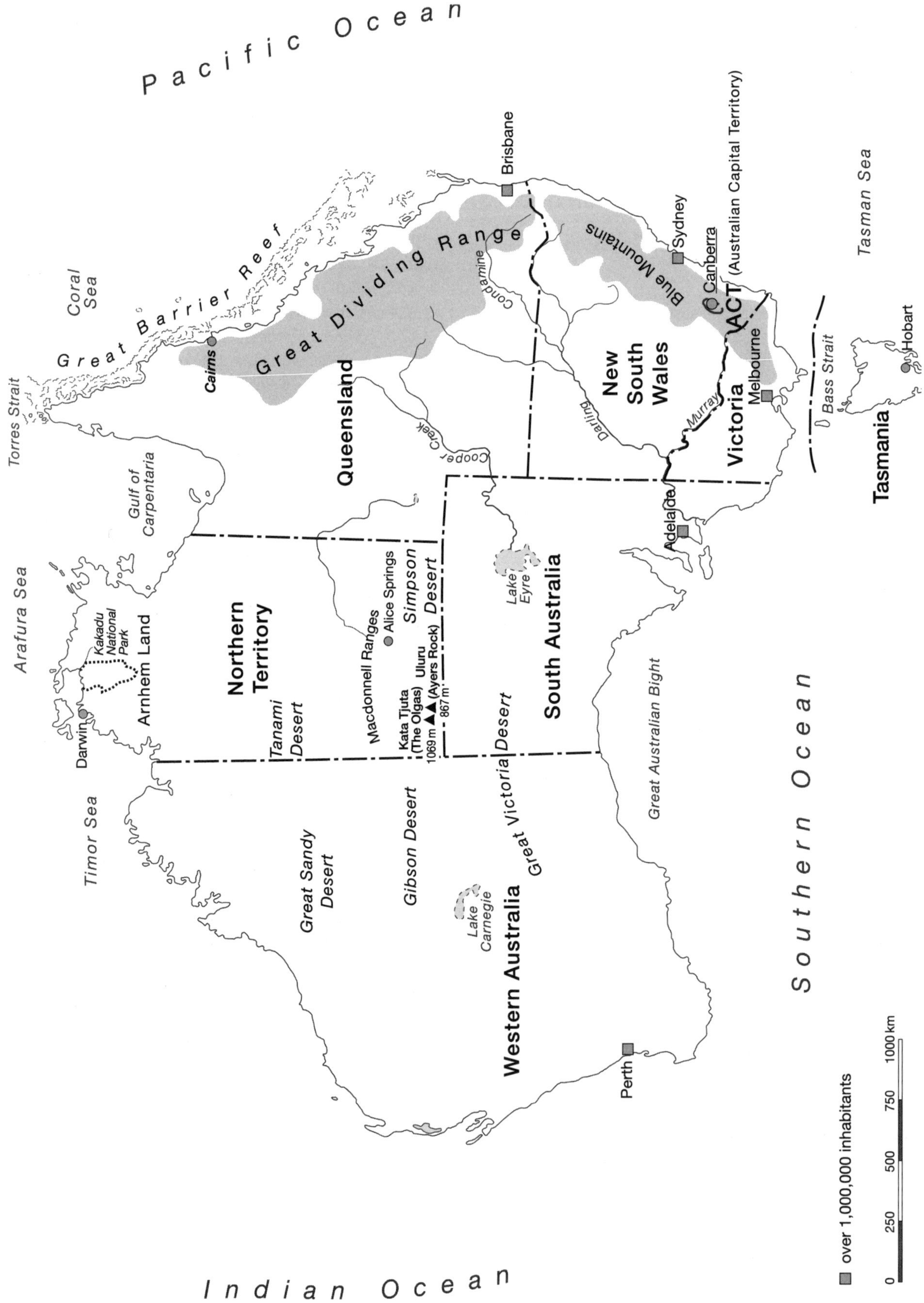

LAUFZETTEL VON: ______________________________

Die folgenden Stationen habe ich schon geschafft:

AUSTRALIA – DOWN UNDER!

- Read the text "Australia – Down Under!"
- Look up any new words in your dictionary. Write the new words in your exercise book.
- Take the map of Australia and try to find Brisbane, Melbourne, Sydney, Canberra, Perth, the Blue Mountains and the Great Barrier Reef.

Materials: dictionary, exercise book, map of Australia

AUSTRALIA – DOWN UNDER!

Did you know: Australia is the only country that is also a continent. Australia is full of extremes: it has both tropical jungles and huge deserts. More than three-quarters of Australia is unwelcoming wilderness. There are six major deserts, but as an island surrounded by water, Australia also has many beaches: around 7,000!

Australia is famous for its "outback", the wilderness in the heart of the country. Not many people live there – it is too hot, too dry and too harsh for most people. Most Australians live along the coast in cities or towns. Most of the bigger cities are on the eastern and southern coasts. The biggest cities are Brisbane, Sydney, Melbourne, Adelaide, and Perth. Australia's capital city is called Canberra. Only 20 per cent of Australians live in the country, which is known in Australia as "the bush". All in all, only around 19 million people live in Australia, even though it is the sixth largest country in the world – (compare this to the relatively small island of Great Britain which has a population of around 60 million).

In eastern Australia you find mostly grasslands, which are used for sheep and cattle farms. There are also mountainous areas in Australia. Look at the map and see if you can find the Blue Mountains: They got their name because of the blue clouds made by eucalyptus trees. The trees give off tiny drops of oil which make the air shine blue. Eucalyptus trees are also fire-resistant! This way they can survive the many bushfires in Australia.

Summer starts in December, autumn in March, winter in June and spring in September. Spending Christmas at the beach or skiing in August may seem strange but Australia's seasons are the opposite of the northern hemisphere. Australia's weather depends very much on where you are: It can be freezing cold in the mountains and burning hot in the deserts. Along the coastal regions where most people live, temperatures are not extreme.

WEATHER WORDS – WORKSHEET I

Australia has deserts, tropical rainforests, high mountains, endless grasslands and countless beaches: This means you need a lot of words to describe Australian weather.

- Look up any words you don't know.
- Write the words into the mindmap.
- Compare your solution with the mindmap example.

Materials: dictionary

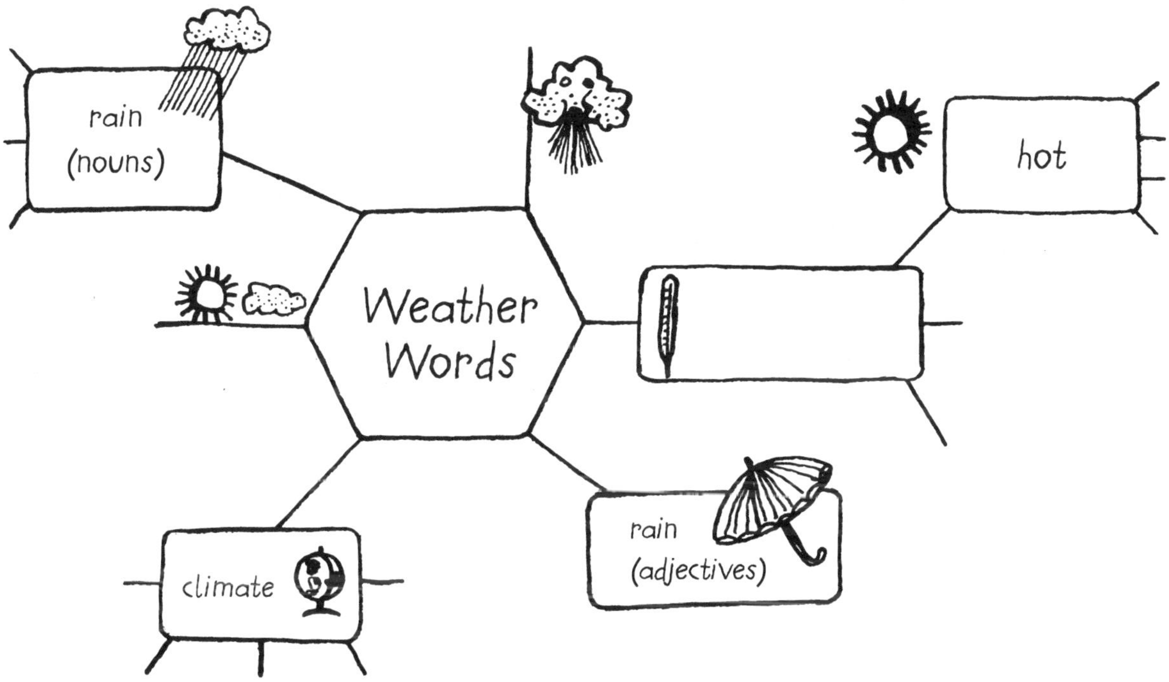

antarctic baking blizzard boiling breeze bright chilly cloudy
cool downpour drizzle dry fine freezing frosty gale gust
overcast rainy scorching shower storm subtropical mild sun or cloud
sunny temperate temperature thunderstorm tropical warm wind

WEATHER WORDS – WORKSHEET II

Let's find more weather words and phrases using the Internet.

- Type in "weather" into the search field of the online dictionary http://dict.leo.org. Look at the new words listed there.
- Make another mindmap in your exercise book with new weather words and phrases you find.

Materials: computer with Internet access

WEATHER WORDS – EXAMPLE

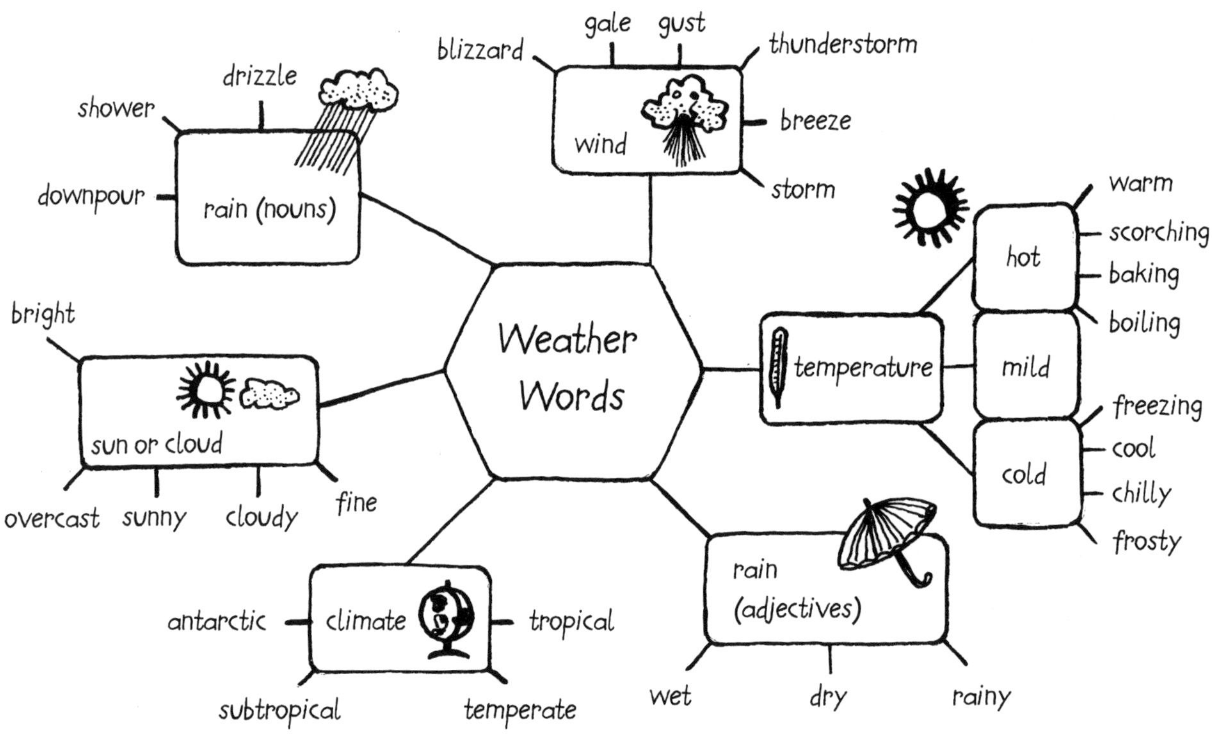

WHERE TO GO IN AUSTRALIA

- In the text below some definite articles ("the") are missing. Fill in the missing articles where they are needed. If no article is needed, write ✘.
- Compare your solutions with the answer key.
- Look at the map of Australia again. Draw the outline of Australia in your exercise book and make a map of the journey.

Note: Here are some rules to help you decide if you need to use "the" or not:

Normally, you say "the"

- ▷ with regions
  example: the south of Australia
- ▷ with mountains if you mean more than one
  example: the Rocky Mountains
- ▷ when you mean something specific
  example: She has found the love of her life. (But: She is in love.)

Normally you don't say "the"

- ▷ with the names of continents
  example: Africa (not: the Africa)
- ▷ with cities/towns/villages
  example: Sydney (not: the Sydney)
- ▷ when you mean something in general
  example: I don't like spiders. (Not: the spiders)

WHERE TO GO IN AUSTRALIA

Australia is a place like no other. Where else can you get dangerously close to a crocodile, visit rainforests, drive through deserts and spend some time on the most beautiful beaches? You just need to know where to find them!

Let's go on a tour of ______ Australian continent. ______ Australia is divided into eight states.

We want to start our journey in ______ Sydney. Here you can visit famous sights, like ______ famous opera house. ______ Blue Mountains are near Sydney. From here let's go north and see ______ rainforests in Queensland. Fly to ______ Darwin in ______ north of Australia. From there you can explore ______ wonderful Kakadu National Park. Then fly south to ______ Alice Springs. From this famous outback town, it is only a short trip to ______ most famous of Australian sights: Ayers Rock. From ______ Alice Springs fly to ______ Perth to see ______ west. Sorry, there is so much more to see, but you have to go back to Sydney and catch a flight home.

Materials: exercise book, map of Australia

OFF TO AUSTRALIA I

You're going on a trip to Australia!

RULES

- ▷ Play with your classmates. One of you should watch the time.
- ▷ Throw the dice and move the correct number of spaces.
- ▷ Talk about the topic on the space each time you land on a new one. Keep talking in English for at least 15 seconds. If your answer was shorter you have to move back three spaces.
- ▷ If you land on an action space pick up an action card, read it out loud and follow the instructions.
- ▷ If you land on a question space pick up a question card and read out the question to the other players. The person who says the answer first moves forward one space.

Materials: board, dice, counters (= Spielsteine; e. g. rubbers, pencil sharpeners), action cards, question cards, watch

ACTION CARDS

Congratulations! You have won a flight to Sydney. Move forward three spaces.	You are travelling in the outback and forgot to take water with you. Go back to "START".	You want to watch some kangaroos. Miss a turn.
You have forgotten your suitcase at the airport. Move back two spaces.	Your hotel in Perth is booked out. Stay where you are for another round.	You have been invited to visit a sheep farm in Western Australia. Move forward two spaces.
You want to go surfing but you are nowhere near a beach. Move forward one space.	You have seen your first kangaroo in the wild! Hop forward one space.	You have been caught in a thunderstorm in the Blue Mountains. Miss a turn.
Your flight to Tasmania has been cancelled. Go back three spaces.	You are sunbathing on Bondi Beach in Sydney. Miss a turn.	You are running away from a big hairy spider. Move forward three spaces.

OFF TO AUSTRALIA II

QUESTION CARDS

Look at the map of Australia and find out: What is the Great Dividing Range? **A long stretch of mountains in western Australia**	Look at the map of Australia and find out: How high is Ayers Rock (Uluru)? **867 metres**	What is the capital city of Australia? **Canberra**
Look at the map of Australia and find out: What state is Ayers Rock (Uluru) in? **Northern Territory**	Look at the map of Australia and find out: What state is Canberra in? **Australian Capital Territory**	What is Tasmania? **An Australian state and an island**
Look at the map of Australia and find out: Which is the largest Australian state? **Western Australia**	Where do most Australians live? **On the east coast**	Look at the map of Australia and find out: What state is Alice Springs in? **Northern Territory**
How many states does Australia have? **Eight**	Look at the map of Australia and find out: Where is the Great Barrier Reef? **In the Pacific Ocean on the north-eastern coast**	Look at the map of Australia and find out: Which are Australia's five largest cities? **Brisbane, Sydney, Melbourne, Adelaide, Perth**

OFF TO AUSTRALIA – BOARD

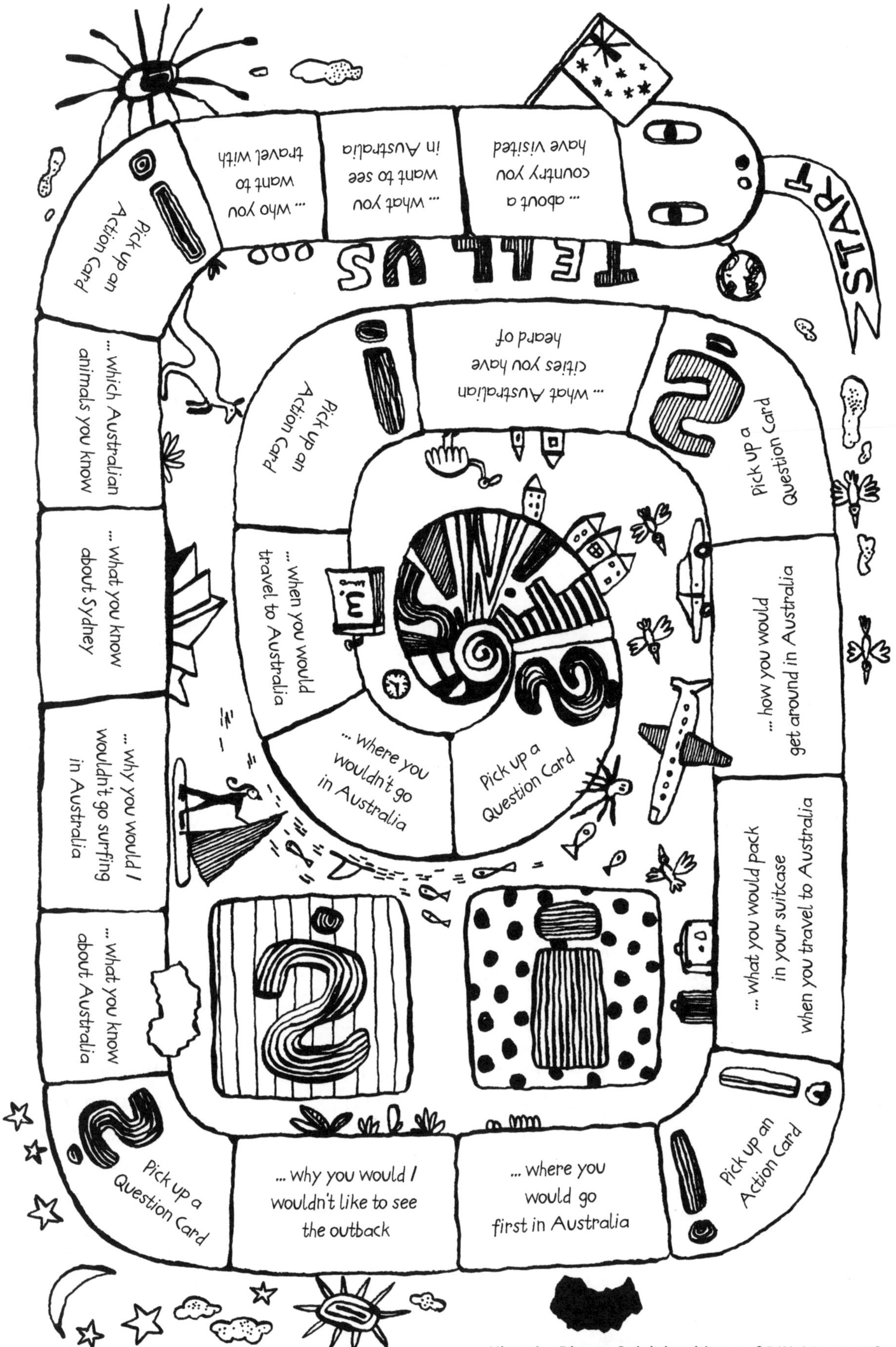

Hinweis: Diesen Spielplan bitte auf DIN A3 vergrößern.

AUSTRALIA DAY

- Put the paragraphs of the text "Australia Day" in the right order. Check your solution with the answer key. Glue the text into your exercise book.
- Look up any new words in your dictionary. Write the new words in your exercise book.
- Find a separate title for each paragraph. Compare your solution with the answer key.

Materials: dictionary, exercise book, glue

AUSTRALIA DAY

For many millions of years, Australia was cut off from the rest of the world. The first humans travelled across the sea from Indonesia about 70,000 years ago. Australia's original inhabitants are called the Australian Aborigines.

The first Europeans ever to reach Australia were Dutch traders and Dutch and English pirates. But in the 18th century, the continent was still almost unknown to Europeans, until the English explorer James Cook sailed towards Australia.

On 19 April 1770, Cook's sailors sighted the Australian coast. They went ashore and were surprised: They were surrounded by hundreds of completely unknown plants and animals. When their ship sailed a bit further up the coast, something terrible happened: it was badly damaged by a huge coral reef. It took a long time to repair the ship, but in the end, a year after the accident, the explorers were safely back in England.

While the ship was being repaired, both sailors and scientists, who had come along too, had a lot of time to explore the new land. They were most amazed by an extraordinary animal: It stood on two hind legs. It made long, big jumps! And what was most exciting of all: From a large pocket on the stomach of the mother animal appeared the little face of a baby animal. Yes, for the first time, Europeans were looking at a kangaroo.

On 22 August 1770, Cook claimed all eastern of Australia for the English King George III. Back home, the explorers suggested that prisoners could be taken to Australia. English prisons were extremely full, and Australia was a vast and empty space! Australia's first European settlement was founded on 26 January 1778. 26 January has become the day Australians celebrate the founding of the Australian nation.

Many Australian Aborigines however, do not celebrate Australia Day. For them, this date means the sad beginning of the end of their traditional way of life.

EXPLORING WORDS

In the text "Australia Day" (Station 2 A) there are a lot of words that you can change to make new ones.

- Fill in the missing words in the table below.
- Look up the words you need in a dictionary.
- Compare your solutions with the answer key.

Materials: dictionary

verb	**person noun**	**abstract noun**
explore	*explorer*	*exploration*
	discoverer	
		settlement
imprison		
		travel
	finder	
found		
		origin
———		history

HISTORY BLOCKBUSTERS

Active or passive? In this game, you have to turn active sentences into passive sentences.

For example: ACTIVE: The explorer James Cook **claimed** Australia.

PASSIVE: Australia **was claimed** by the explorer James Cook.

- Play with two teams plus a referee (= Schiedsrichter).
- The first team picks any letter from the blockbusters grid. The referee reads out the corresponding sentence on the list. The first team turns the active sentence into a passive sentence.
- If the sentence is right, the team marks the letter with their colour. Now the second team picks a letter.
- If a team gets the sentence wrong, the other team has a go at giving the correct answer.
- If both teams get it wrong, the referee reads out the answer. No team can win this letter now.
- Continue until one team has coloured a complete line either vertically or horizontally.

Materials: blockbusters grid, blockbusters sentences, rules, coloured pencils

BLOCKBUSTERS GRID

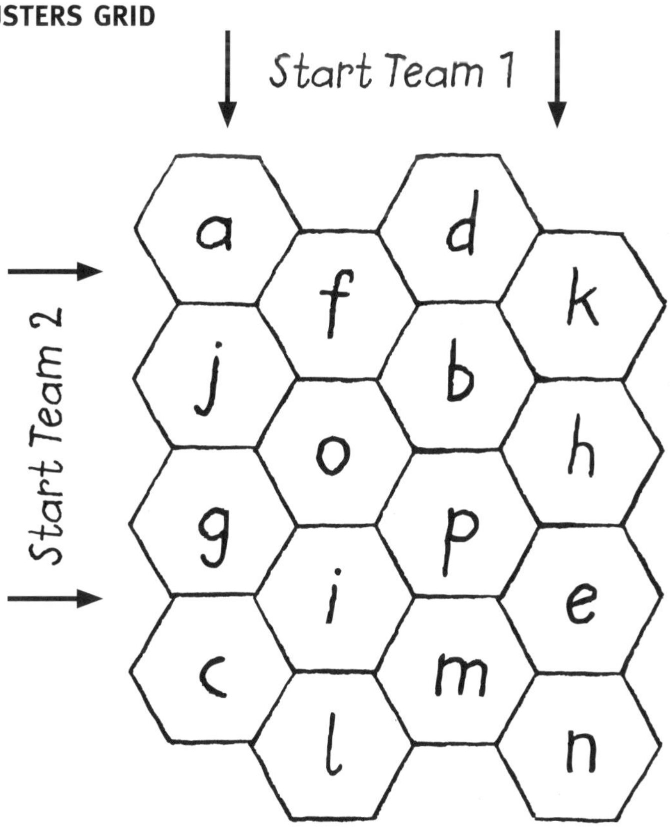

HISTORY BLOCKBUSTERS – SENTENCES

	ACTIVE	PASSIVE
a	Scientists study Aboriginal history.	Aboriginal history is studied by scientists.
b	The first humans used fire to hunt animals.	Fire was used by the first humans to hunt animals.
c	Europeans made the first maps of Australia.	The first maps of Australia were made by Europeans.
d	In 1606, Europeans reached Australia for the first time.	In 1606, Australia was reached by Europeans for the first time.
e	Australian Aborigines used boomerangs to hunt for food.	Boomerangs were used by Australian Aborigines to hunt for food.
f	Captain James Cook claimed Australia for Great Britain in 1770.	Australia was claimed for Great Britain by Captain James Cook in 1770.
g	Cook's explorers found many new plants.	Many new plants were found by Cook's explorers.
h	Kangaroos surprised the scientists.	The scientists were surprised by kangaroos.
i	Sailors had to repair Cook's ship.	Cook's ship had to be repaired by sailors.
j	English soldiers took English prisoners to Australia.	English prisoners were taken to Australia by English soldiers.
k	Prisoners set up the first settlement in Australia.	The first settlement in Australia was set up by prisoners.
l	The English king sent prisoners to Australia.	Prisoners were sent to Australia by the English king.
m	On January 26, many Australians celebrate Australia Day.	On January 26, Australia Day is celebrated by many Australians.
n	Australians raise many flags on Australia Day.	Many flags are raised by Australians on Australia Day.
o	Many Australian Aborigines do not celebrate Australia Day.	Australia Day is not celebrated by many Australian Aborigines.
p	Europeans killed many Aborigines.	Many Aborigines were killed by Europeans.

AUSTRALIAN LEGEND

You and your friend are visiting an Australian tourist attraction in Glenrowan – the place where the Australian hero Ned Kelly fought his last battle. You are listening to the tourist guide, when some Germans come up to you. They ask if you could help them understand what the guide is saying.

- Listen to the cassette.
- Translate text A to your friend, your partner translates text B.
- Write the whole translation in your exercise book.
- Compare your solution with the answer key.

Materials: cassette recorder, cassette, exercise book

NED KELLY'S LAST BATTLE IN GLENROWAN

TEXT A

Ned Kelly is Australia's Robin Hood. He was liked by the poor and fought by the police. He led a criminal life. He robbed banks and he stole cattle from rich farmers.

He was an extremely good rider, and he often won battles against policemen together with his gang. He was protected by a helmet and a suit of armour that he had made himself.

TEXT B

Here in Glenrowan he fought his last battle which lasted long into the night. He fought a lot of policemen on that day. He was only defeated when the policemen noticed that his legs were unprotected, and they shot him in the legs.

He was only 25 years old when he was finally caught. He was hanged on November 11, 1880 in Melbourne.

SEARCH AUSTRALIA

When you do an Internet search, you type in keywords into the search field of a search engine (www.google.de). Finding the right keywords is important for a successful Internet search. You can use more than one keyword at a time.

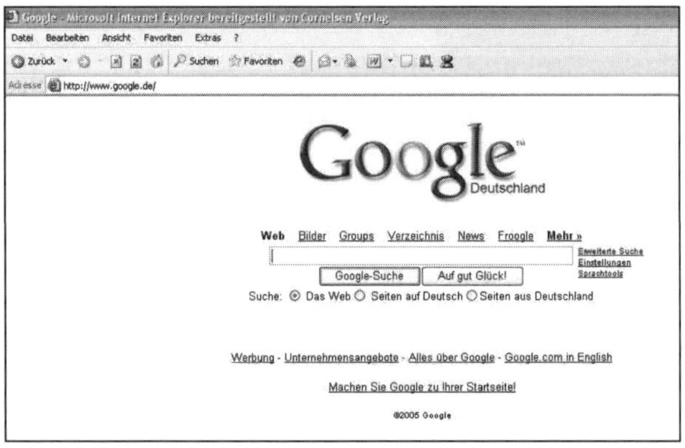

- Fill in the missing keywords below.
- Compare your solution with the answer key.
- Now use the computer. Try out different keywords to find out more about Australian explorers. Take notes in your exercise book. Write down which keywords worked best.

Materials: computer with Internet access, exercise book

CHOOSING THE RIGHT KEYWORDS

- You might have to find a different word for your topic.
- *Write down keywords that mean more or less the **same** as the words below:*

shore → ______________________________

traveller → ______________________________

- You might have to find a word that has a wider meaning than your topic.
- *Write down keywords that have a **wider** meaning than the words below:*

kangaroo → ______________________________

surfing → ______________________________

- You might have to find a word that has a narrower meaning than your topic.
- *Write down keywords that have a **narrower** meaning than the words below:*

history → ______________________________

flora → ______________________________

ABORIGINAL AUSTRALIA I

- Read the text "Aboriginal Australia".
- Look up any new words in your dictionary. Write the new words in your exercise book.

Materials: dictionary, exercise book, computer with Internet access, printer, paper, poster, markers, scissors, glue

ABORIGINAL AUSTRALIA

Australian Aborigines were the first people to inhabit Australia. Their ancestors arrived in Australia at least 50,000 years ago – some historians say it might even have been as long as 150,000 years ago. The Australian Aborigines were hunter-gatherers for most of their history. When Australia became British in 1770, their lives changed dramatically. They lost most of their land and the white settlers in some parts of Australia were allowed to shoot them like animals.

In the early 20th century, many Aboriginal families were separated from each other. By order of the Australian government, white Australians took Aboriginal children from their mothers, so they would grow up in white families and forget their own culture. Aborigines now have the same rights as white Australians, but they are still disadvantaged. In 1998 Australians held the first "National Sorry Day" – the Australian people apologised for all the horrors that had happened to the Aborigines.

Much of traditional Aboriginal culture is based on "the Dreaming" or "Dreamtime". The Dreaming is the way traditional Aboriginal people explain life and how the world came into being. The Dreaming is told in songs, dances and paintings. Aboriginal paintings show many circles, curved and straight lines, or the tracks of animals. Circles often stand for "waterhole", "camp site" or "important place". Curved lines stand for "rain" or "water travelling underground". A C-shaped figure might mean a "person". Australian didgeridoos are often decorated with such symbols.

ABORIGINAL AUSTRALIA II

Some Aboriginal symbols found in traditional artwork:

boomerang

adult

child

emu

place

spears

kangaroo

honey ant

digging stick

bush plum

- Create a poster about Australian Aborigines. It should include information on their history and their culture.
- Use the Internet to find out more facts about Australian Aborigines. You can do your own search by using a search engine (e.g. http://www.google.de). You can also look at the websites listed under "Useful links".
- On your poster you should try to say what a didgeridoo is, who invented it, what it looks like, how it is made and how you play it.
- Present your poster to the class.

Useful links:

http://aboriginalart.com.au

http://en.wikipedia.org/wiki/Didgeridoo

http://www.didgeridooing.com/gallery1.htm

IN THE NEWS

Let's look at some useful words for talking about the news.

- Unscramble the words below and write down the correct words.
- Compare your solutions with the answer key.

1 RORTRPEE — A person whose job is to discover information about news events and describe them for a newspaper or magazine or for radio or television: ______________________________

2 VEWNEITIR — A meeting in which someone is asked questions about themselves for a newspaper article, television show, etc: ______________________________

3 LNIEHEDA — A line of words printed in large letters as the title of a story in a newspaper, or the main points of the news that are broadcast on television or radio: ______________________________

4 NFGOIRE NERSOCOPTNRED — A person employed by a newspaper, a television station, etc. to send reports from a foreign country (two words): ______________________________

5 RADBOACTS — A television or radio programme: ______________________________

6 HAERETW SETROAFC — A statement of what the weather is likely to be for the next day, usually broadcast on television or radio or printed in a newspaper (two words): ______________________________

7 TILRACE — A piece of writing on a particular subject in a newspaper or magazine: ______________________________

SCHOOL OF THE AIR

Violet Radcliffe is 15 years old and lives on an outback sheep station in Queensland, Australia – several hundred miles away from the nearest school.

- Listen to the tape without looking at the worksheet.
- Now read the text "School of the air". Listen to the tape again and fill in the missing words. Decide if the word is a plural word or has a genitive 's.
- Compare your solution with the answer key.
- Rewind the tape when you are done!

Materials: cassette, cassette recorder, worksheet

NOTE: the boy**'s** school → refers to one boy and his school (singular genitive)
the boy**s'** school → refers to several boys and their school (plural genitive)
the boy**s** → refers to several boys (plural)

SCHOOL OF THE AIR

Hi there!

My name is Violet Radcliffe. I am 15 ________ old. My family and I live on a sheep station in the outback in Queensland, which is why I am a pupil at Mount Isa School of the air. Normal schools are too far away so I have to work at home. I have a teacher who talks to me and my class through the radio for an hour or so every day. We use high frequency ________, so I can talk to everyone in my class. There are ten of us, and ________________ home is a sheep or cattle station. Sometimes we all meet. We have a ________ day in Mount Isa once every year, when the whole school comes together, even people who live 800 km away! After our lesson our teacher will set us some exercises, and she calls us on the phone later in the day to talk about our ________ work. My teacher comes and visits me from time to time which is nice. Our ________________ library is very important to me. I use it a lot. The librarian sends us the books we need by post. We have all the subjects that normal ________________ have as well. I learn German as a foreign language!

LIFE ON A SHEEP STATION

You are going to produce a short radio interview about life in the outback. Work with a friend.

- Partner A is the reporter, interviewing Violet Radcliffe, a 15-year-old girl who lives on a sheep station. Write down your questions for Violet in your exercise book.
- Partner B is Violet Radcliffe. Write down your answers.
- In your interview, you should talk about where Violet lives, her school and how she likes it. There are useful words and ideas on the interview sheet. Begin like this: "Hello, this is ... for Radio 5. Today ..."
- Act out the interview together.
- Record the interview on tape. Do not rewind the tape!

Materials: interview worksheet, exercise book, cassette, cassette recorder

Violet
Begrüße den Reporter.
Violet:
Violet:
Violet:
Verabschiede dich.

LIFE ON A SHEEP STATION – INTERVIEW

15-year-old Violet Radcliffe lives on a sheep station and is a school-of-the-air pupil. Here are some ideas for your interview:

G'DAY AUSTRALIA!

- Read the text "G'day Australia!"
- Look up any new words in your dictionary. Write the new words in your exercise book.
- Would you like to spend Christmas watching a sports match? Why (not)? Tell your friend.

Materials: dictionary, exercise book

G'DAY AUSTRALIA

If you visit Australia, be prepared that Australians have their own way of speaking English. Some people call it "Strine". Strine has its own words, like "snag" for "sausage", and shortened words like "barbie" for "barbecue", "mozzie" for "mosquito", "roo" for "kangaroo", "bickie" for "biscuit" or "arvo" for "afternoon". Strine is famous for its expressions that seem typical of the Australian lifestyle. Take this one for example: "He is a snag short of a barbie" is used to describe a person who seems a bit mad – after all, what sort of person tries to have a barbecue without any food, not even a sausage, to put on it?

What else is special about the Australian lifestyle? If you think summer, sun and beaches, you are quite right. Australia wouldn't be Australia without its many beaches. One of the most popular water sports is surfing. Australia was the first place in the world to have surf lifesaving clubs. Every summer, thousands of volunteer lifesavers patrol beaches and provide first-aid when needed.

Another sport that is very popular in Australia, especially in the summer season, is cricket. Cricket is a tiny bit like baseball – although one match can last up to five days! "Batsmen" try to hit the ball as far as they can into the field so they can score points by running while the opposing team gets the ball back. Just in case you are talking to a cricket fan: don't say their favourite game is like baseball – they don't like it!

For many Australian families, cricket plays a big role, especially at Christmas. December 26th always sees the start of an international game at the Melbourne Cricket Ground. 90,000 spectators come and watch it live, many more Australians follow the event on TV.

SPEAK STRINE! – WORKSHEET

Australians have many words and phrases that are different to American and British English.

- Try to match each Australian expression with the correct meaning. The pictures will help you.
- Compare your solutions with the answer key.

1. She is a show-off.	2. He is extremely boring.	3. He is new to surfing.
4. It was expensive.	5. He is extremely angry.	6. She's crazy.
7. She thinks she is the greatest.	8. She is sad and upset.	9. No problem!
10. Everything will be fine.	11. He is extremely busy.	12. This is broken!

A

She has tickets on herself.

B

She's as happy as a boxing kangaroo in fog.

C

She's apples.

D

He is as mad as a cut snake.

E

This is cactus!

F

She's got a roo loose in the top paddock.

G

No worries, mate!

H

He would talk a glass eye to sleep.

I

He is a shark biscuit.

J

She's as flash as a rat with a gold tooth.

K

He's as flat out as a lizard drinking.

L

It cost big bickies.

SPEAK STRINE! – QUIZ

- Play in a group (2 – 4 people can play together). First your group needs to make 12 quiz cards, one for each Australian idiom. Divide the cards equally between you. Copy the expressions from the worksheet, one on each card.
- For each of your cards, think of three possible but **false** explanations of the phrases and write them on the card together with the **correct** explanation. Underline the correct explanation. Don't show your explanations to the other players.

EXAMPLE:

He's as flat out as a lizard drinking.

A: He is thirsty.

B: He has drunk too much alcohol.

C: He is extremely busy.

D: He is tired.

- When all players have finished their cards, the youngest player reads out the first phrase and all four explanations. The player who is the first to choose the correct explanation wins the card.
- The next person, sitting to the left of the first player, reads out the next card.
- The game ends when all cards have been won. The person with the most cards is the winner.

Materials: 12 blank quiz cards per group, Speak Strine worksheet

CHRISTMAS IN THE SUMMER SEASON

- Fill in the right words: *some, any, a lot of, much* or *no*
- Compare your solutions with the answer key.
- Write a letter explaining how you celebrate Christmas.
- Show your letter to your teacher. She/he will correct it.

21 Bradman Crescent
Melbourne
December 16th

Dear Tom!

Thank you for your long letter. You wanted to know how we celebrate Christmas in Australia? Okay, here goes: Santa Claus doesn't get __________ snow here and is better off using a surfboard instead of his sleigh! As far back as I can remember we've always had blue skies and temperatures around 25 degrees Celsius at Christmas.

I just love it. Not just because of the presents. Tomorrow is my last day at school. Christmas means the end of a school year. There's __________ school until after Australia Day (that's on January 26th). We don't have to do __________ homework during the summer holidays – so we can just relax, have picnics, go to the beach ...

At the moment everyone is beginning to get ready for the Christmas parties. My mum has bought __________ new decorations for our Christmas tree. We also hang up __________ twigs of "Christmas bush". It's a plant that grows here with red berries on it. On Christmas Eve we go into town and sing __________ Christmas carols. Thousands of people meet in town, light candles and sing. Later we hang up stockings and leave a cool drink for Santa Claus.

On Christmas day it's presents, presents, presents! Later in the morning we usually have a barbecue in the garden with __________ friends and family. There's so __________ food, you wouldn't believe it. My favourite is Christmas Ice Cream Pudding: That's vanilla ice cream with lots of nuts, dried fruit and chocolate bits mixed in. But let me tell you the best bit: My dad has got us __________ tickets for the cricket again!

That's it for now! Please write soon and tell me how you celebrate Christmas in Germany!

Yours, Mandy

BEACH SAFETY

You are the surf lifesaver at the beach.
A tourist asks you if you can help him understand all the warning signs.

- Try to have a conversation and write the missing sentences on the worksheet. Compare your solution with the answer key.
- Act out the conversation with a friend.

Materials: dictionary

(!) Remember: **shall** = sollen; **may** = dürfen; **must** = müssen; **mustn't** = nicht dürfen

Swim between red and yellow flags

Do not enter the water

Beware of strong currents

Beware of high surf

Beware of hazardous marine creatures

Bombing prohibited

TOURIST	**YOU**
Hi there! Can you help me please?	Frage, ob du ihm die Warnschilder erklären sollst.
Yes, please. I'm not sure where I'm allowed to swim.	
	Erkläre ihm nun in einfachen Worten, worauf er beim Schwimmen besonders achten muss.
Okay, thank you!	

WALTZING MATILDA

"Waltzing Matilda" is a much loved Australian song. Some call it Australia's unofficial national anthem (= inoffizielle Nationalhymne). You are going to use the Internet to find out what it is all about.

- Listen to the song and then read through the text. All the words in bold print (= fett gedruckt) are Australian words.
- Guess what the words mean and write down your guesses on the "Waltzing Matilda Worksheet".
- Find out what the words really mean by typing them into the search field of an Internet search engine (e.g. http://www.google.de).
- Write down the explanation of the words on the worksheet.
- Write down what the song is about.
- Compare your answers with the answer key. Then listen to the song again!

Materials: computer with Internet access, worksheet

WALTZING MATILDA – TEXT

Once a jolly **swagman** camped by a **billabong**
Under the shade of a **coolibah tree**
And he sang as he watched and waited 'til his **billy** boiled
You'll come a-waltzing matilda with me

Waltzing matilda, waltzing matilda
You'll come a waltzing matilda with me
And he sang as he watched and waited 'til his billy boiled
You'll come a-waltzing matilda with me

Down came a **jumbuck** to drink at that billabong
Up jumped the swagman and grabbed him with glee
And he sang as he stuffed that jumbuck in his tucker-bag
You'll come a-waltzing matilda with me

Chorus

Up rode the **squatter**, mounted on his thoroughbred
Up rode the **troopers**, one, two, three
"Where's that jolly jumbuck you've got in your **tucker-bag**?"
You'll come a-waltzing matilda with me

Chorus

Up jumped the swagman and sprang into that billabong
"You'll never take me alive!", said he
And his ghost may be heard as you pass by that billabong
You'll come a-waltzing matilda with me

Chorus

Listen to parts of the song here:
http://www.songsforteaching.com/folk/waltzingmatilda.htm

WALTZING MATILDA – WORKSHEET

■ Guess what the words and the song could mean.
Then look up the words on the Internet and write down their meaning.

Waltzing Matilda: Words	Your guess	Your research
swagman		
billabong		
coolibah tree		
billy		
waltzing matilda		
jumbuck		
tucker-bag		
squatter		
troopers		
THE SONG IS ABOUT:		

IN THE OUTBACK

- Read the text "In the Outback".
- Look up any new words in your dictionary. Write the new words in your exercise book.
- Look through travel brochures of Australia and make a collage about the outback using information from the text.

Materials: dictionary, exercise book, travel brochures, paper, scissors, glue

IN THE OUTBACK

The Australian outback is also called "the never-never" or "the back of beyond" – an area which is far away from civilization. It is difficult to say where exactly the outback begins and where it ends. For most Australians, the outback refers to the huge deserts in the heart of the country with their characteristic red sand.
There are many popular tourist attractions in the outback. The most popular of them all is Ayers Rock, or Uluru, as the Aborigines call it. It is a huge rock in central Australia, more than 860 metres high. Depending on the time of day and the weather, the rock changes its colour and can glow blue, or violet, or in all shades of red. The Aborigines believe that it is inhabited by spirits and to them the rock is sacred.
If you want to travel through the outback, it is very important that you prepare your journey well. Always tell someone about your route and when you plan to be back. Make sure you have enough spare petrol for long distances. Take plenty of water with you and enough food. You need a high-frequency radio in case your car breaks down. Mobile phones don't reach far enough. In case of an emergency stay near your car in the shade and wait for help. Most problems in the outback happen when people go to look for help. It is much safer to wait for Australia's famous Royal Flying Doctor Service. This is why you need a high-frequency radio: In the outback you can contact doctors with it, and they can help quickly because they use planes as ambulances.

OUTBACK – SURVIVAL WORDS

- Look at the picture.
- Try to find the words for the nine numbered things and write them in your exercise book.
- Compare your words with the answer key.
- Think of more "travel/survival" words and write them in your exercise book.

Materials: dictionary, exercise book

EMERGENCY IN THE OUTBACK

A doctor from the flying doctor service is telling you about his last emergency call.

- Listen to the tape.
- Put the sentences in the right order. Once they are in the right order, the letters at the beginning of each sentence spell a word.
- Write down the sentences in reported speech.

  Example:

  "I answered an emergency call." → He said that he had answered an emergency call.

  Remember:

  Personal pronouns and the tense of the sentence change:

  Example: "**I** *answered*" → **He** said he *had answered.*

  You need to use reporting verbs from time to time:

  Example: to say, to explain, to ask, to report, to add, to conclude ...
- Compare your text with the answer key.

Materials: cassette, cassette-recorder, sentences, exercise book

A	"I rescued a family; there were four people: two parents and a boy and a girl."
Y	"I found them next to their car."
E	"The family was suffering because they hadn't prepared their journey very well."
R	"Luckily they brought a lot of water, but they forgot to bring a radio."
S	"They tried to use their mobile phone to call for help but it didn't work."
R	"They had to wait five days until someone found them."
O	"Their water supply was used up, and the children were very weak."
C	"My partner and I got there just in time. They are fine now."
K	"It is important to always carry a radio in the outback."

RESCUED BY THE FLYING DOCTOR SERVICE

You are a reporter for a newspaper. Your are writing a news report about the Carters, a family who were stranded in the outback.

- Write the report in your exercise book. The pictures and words below will help you.
- In your report you should sometimes use direct speech and sometimes reported speech to report what the Carter family told you.

  Example for direct speech:

  "The car broke down," said Mr Carter.

  Example for reported speech:

  Mr Carter said that the car had broken down.
- Show your text to your teacher. He or she will correct it.
- Start your report like this: "Adelaide. Last Thursday, a family of four became stranded in the outback ...".

Materials: exercise book

SIGHTSEEING IN SYDNEY

Let's go on a sightseeing tour of Sydney, Australia's most famous city.

- Try to find the sights listed below on http://www.australianexplorer.com/sydney_sights.htm
- Add two Sydney sights you find interesting: There is a list of sights on the left under "Sydney info".
- Make notes about the sites.
- Make your own tourist guide of Sydney! Print out pictures of the sights, cut them out and glue them into your exercise book and write down some of the information you found on the Internet. To print out pictures you need to click on the right mouse button, and then click on "Bild drucken". You can find a lot of pictures if you go to http://www.google.de. Click on "Bilder" and type in the name of the sight. Ask your teacher if you need help.

Materials: computer with Internet access, printer, paper, scissors, glue, exercise book

Sydney Sights	Your notes
Sydney Opera House	
Sydney Harbour Bridge	
Sydney Harbour	

DEADLY CREATURES

- Read the text.
- Look up any new words and write them down in your exercise book.
- Think of three quiz questions and answers. Write each question on a separate card. Write the correct answers on the question cards.
- Find a partner. Ask each other your quiz questions.
- The person who got the most answers right is the winner.

Materials: dictionary, exercise book, cards

DEADLY CREATURES

If you think of Australia's wildlife, you will probably think first of cute koalas or hopping kangaroos. However, Australia's fauna isn't only famous for these loveable creatures, but also for its extremely dangerous animals. Have you ever heard of the most poisonous animal on earth, the box jellyfish? Well, here is the place to find out more about it.

Box jellyfish can be found in the waters near the North Australian coast. They have large transparent bodies shaped like a box. They carry strong poison in their long tentacles. They are extremely dangerous: no other animal's poison can kill a human in less than four minutes. The poison on their tentacles is so strong that the few people who have survived contact with it describe it as like a powerful electric shock. Box jellyfish have caused more deaths in Australia than snakes, sharks and salt water crocodiles put together. The reason for this is that they are hard to see and their poison comes from all their long tentacles, which means that it can enter the victim's body at different parts at the same time. The effects are so painful that swimmers who brush against the tentacles often don't make it back to the shore to take the antidote. The only way of protecting yourself against box jelly fish is to only swim in safely netted areas or to wear protective clothing.

And there are the snakes and spiders. Australia has hundreds of different species, and quite a lot of them are deadly. However, even though Australia's most poisonous snake, the taipan, has enough poison to kill 100 grown men, it is not half as dangerous as the box jellyfish, because in most cases there is enough time to take the antidote. A person will die only if a snake bite is untreated for several hours. This is also true for spider bites.

This all sounds very frightening, doesn't it? But the truth is, most of Australia's poisonous animals do not want to attack humans. So enjoy Australia's great outdoors, just be careful where you swim or where you sit down!

ANIMAL WORDS – TRIMINO BOARD

Try to match each animal with the correct body part and movement.

- Each picture on the big triangle corresponds with one of the animals listed below. Match the name of the animal with each picture. Look up any new words and animals.
- On one side of a small triangle a sentence begins with a body part of an animal, and the sentence finishes with the animal's movement on another triangle. Put the triangles together so you can read the whole sentence.
- If you put all the triangles together correctly they will fit exactly into the big triangle. Each sentence will cover the picture of corresponding animal.

Materials: trimino board, trimino cards, dictionary

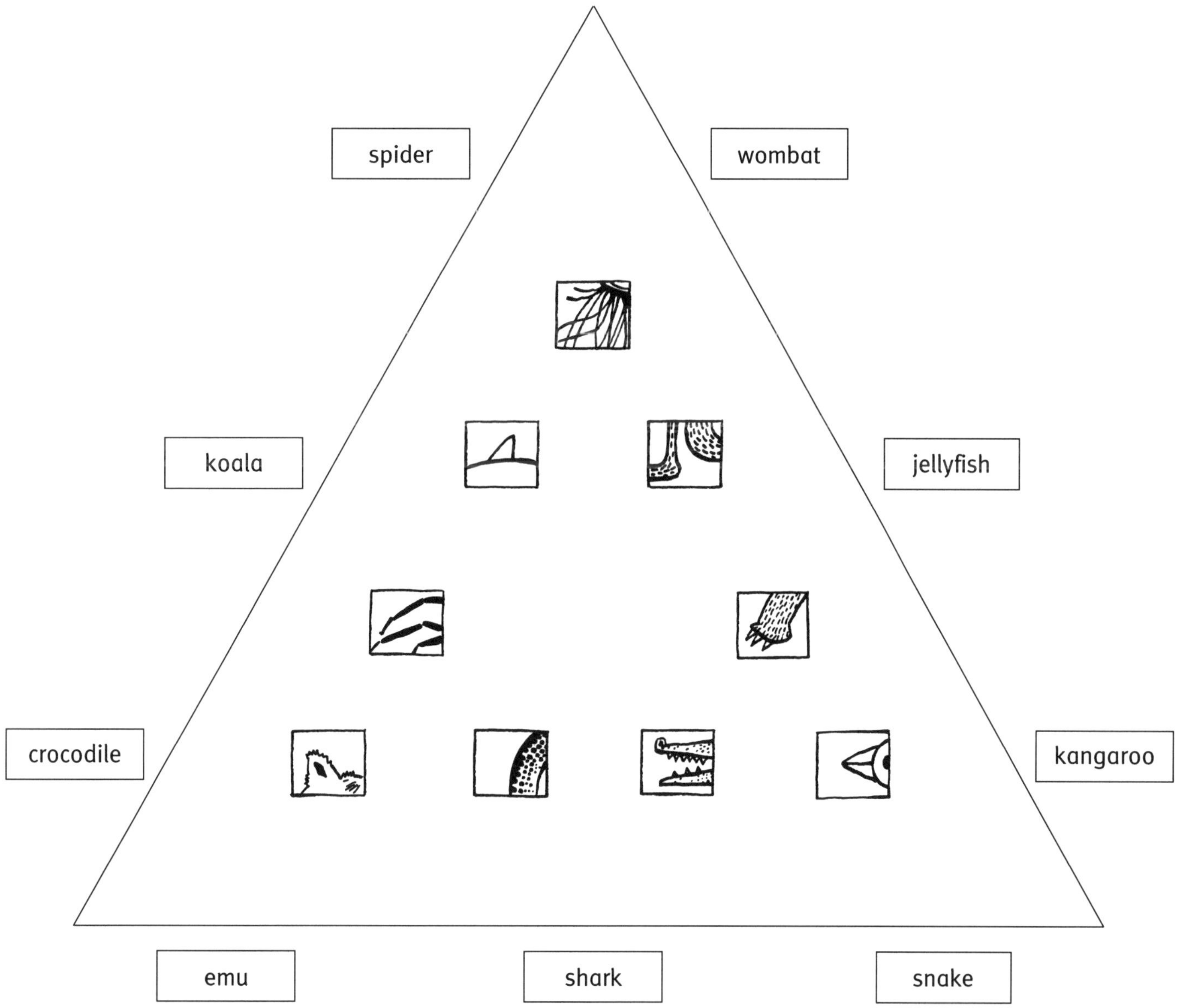

ANIMAL WORDS – TRIMINO CARDS

It has tentacles and floats.

It has fins and swims.

It has a pouch and hops.

It has eight legs and crawls.

It has claws and burrows.

It has fur and climbs.

It has scales and slithers.

It has a tail and paddles.

It has feathers and runs.

ANIMAL TRUMPS

- Fill in the table below.
- Compare your solutions with the answer key.

Remember:
Words with one syllable *-er, -est*
Words with three or more syllables *more, the most*
Words with two syllables ***either** -er, -est **or** more, the most*

Materials: worksheet, dictionary

Adjective	Comparative	Superlative
dangerous	**more** dangerous	**the most** dangerous
fast	fast**er**	the fast**est**
poisonous		
long		
aggressive		
big		
speedy		

ANIMAL TRUMPS – RULES

▷ Play with one, two or three partners. Up to four people can play.
▷ Mix and share out the cards. Each player holds the cards so he/she can only read the top card.
▷ The youngest player starts. He/she chooses a category from the top card, e.g. "Speed" and says: "My animal is faster than yours. Its speed is 45 kilometres per hour."
▷ The player to the right answers e.g. "No, mine is faster than yours. Its speed is 70 kilometres per hour." Or: "Yes, yours is faster than mine." The player with the highest value (= Wert) has to say: "Mine is the fastest." The player who has the top value wins all the cards and puts them at the bottom of his pile of cards. The winner of the round always chooses the next category from the next top card.
▷ If two or more cards have the same top value, or if there is a question mark for that category, all cards of that round are placed in the middle of the table. The same player chooses again from the next card. The winner of the round wins the cards in the middle as well. The person with all the cards at the end is the winner.

Materials: trump cards

ANIMAL TRUMPS – CARDS

KOALA

Max. Speed **3.6** km/h
Size **78** cm
Poison Factor **0**
Aggression Factor **1**
Lifespan **10** years

RED KANGAROO

Max. Speed **70** km/h
Size **1.6** m
Poison Factor **0**
Aggression Factor **3**
Lifespan **6 – 8** years

BOX JELLYFISH

Max. Speed **7.4** km/h
Size **20** cm
Poison Factor **15**
Aggression Factor **5**
Lifespan **6** months

WOMBAT

Max. Speed **40** km/h
Size **100** cm
Poison Factor **0**
Aggression Factor **3**
Lifespan: **5 – 25** years

RED-BACKED SPIDER

Max. Speed **1** km/h
Size **3** cm
Poison Factor **10**
Aggression Factor **2**
Lifespan **2** years

SALTWATER CROCODILE

Max. Speed **11** km/h
Size **4 – 7** m
Poison Factor **0**
Aggression Factor **14**
Lifespan **60** years

LONG-NOSED BANDICOOT

Max. Speed **35** km/h
Size ca. **40** cm
Poison Factor **0**
Aggression Factor **1**
Lifespan **2 – 5** years

EMU

Max. Speed **60** km/h
Size **1.5 – 1.8** m
Poison Factor **0**
Aggression Factor **3**
Lifespan **25 – 30** years

GREAT WHITE SHARK

Max. Speed **24** km/h
Size **3.5 – 5** m
Poison Factor **0**
Aggression Factor **15**
Lifespan **30 – 60** years

ANIMAL TRUMPS – CARDS

FUNNEL-WEB SPIDER

Max. Speed **0.8** km/h
Size **5 – 7** cm
Poison Factor **12**
Aggression Factor **7**
Lifespan (female) **10** years

DINGO

Max. Speed **60** km/h
Size **100** cm
Poison Factor **0**
Aggression Factor **4**
Lifespan **8** years

TIGER SNAKE

Max. Speed **5** km/h
Size **1 – 2** m
Poison Factor **13**
Aggression Factor **2**
Lifespan **?** years

KOOKABURRA

Max. Speed **25** km/h
Size **43** cm
Poison Factor **0**
Aggression Factor **1**
Lifespan **20** years

TASMANIAN DEVIL

Max. Speed **28** km/h
Size **60** cm
Poison Factor **0**
Aggression Factor **5**
Lifespan **8** years

STONEFISH

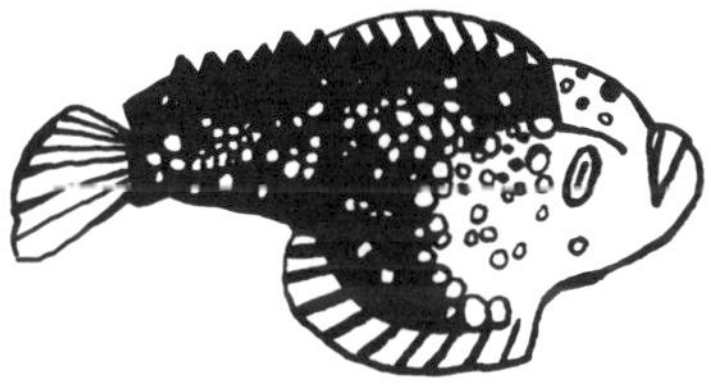

Max. Speed **?** km/h
Size **30** cm
Poison Factor **13**
Aggression Factor **0**
Lifespan **?** years

HUNTSMAN SPIDER

Max. Speed **1.3** km/h
Size **15** cm
Poison Factor **1**
Aggression Factor **5**
Lifespan **2** years

BLUE-RINGED OCTOPUS

Max. Speed **?**
Size: **2 – 20** cm
Poison Factor: **10**
Aggression Factor **0**
Lifespan **2** years

TAIPAN SNAKE

Max. Speed **5** km/h
Size **1.5** m
Poison Factor **15**
Aggression Factor **11**
Lifespan **?** years

WHO'S AFRAID OF SPIDERS?

Are you afraid of spiders? Here is a story about a man who is terrified of them.

- Try to write the story. The pictures and words below will help you.
- Compare your story with the answer key.

Materials: picture story, exercise book

Sunday afternoon – Mr and Mrs Jones at home – Mrs Jones: to knit a pair of socks – Mr Jones: newspaper – cat: asleep in armchair – not go away – Mr Jones: angry – to chase away

Mr Jones: to read – article on most poisonous animals in Australia – cat: angry – Mrs Jones: to feel sorry for – to play with – cat: happy – ball of wool

Cat: to turn round and round – get entangled in the wool – can't free itself – Mrs Jones: to get scissors – to cut loose – Mr Jones: to not notice anything – to carry on reading

Suddenly – Mr Jones: to climb up a bookcase – to shake – to point at black creature – to be very frightened – to refuse to come down

Mrs Jones: to investigate the situation – to pick up black creature – Mr Jones: to warn her – to shout– careful – might be Australia's most poisonous spider – enough poison to kill 60 grown men – could die – no antidote in the house

Mrs Jones: to laugh – to explain – only wool – not poisonous – Mr Jones: relieved – to climb down again – embarrassed – to sit down – cat: triumphant – back in his armchair

THE GREAT BARRIER REEF

The Great Barrier Reef is described by many as the greatest living thing on earth.

- Look up "The Great Barrier Reef" in the Internet encyclopaedia "Wikipedia". Type in http://en.wikipedia.org in the address field of your Internet browser, then type in "Great Barrier Reef" in the search field.
- Find out facts about the Great Barrier Reef. Where is it? What is it? How big is it? Who was the first European explorer to see it? What causes damage to it? Take notes.
- Compare your solutions with the answer key.
- Click on the link "Photos of the Great Barrier Reef – Terra Galleria" at the bottom of the Wikipedia article on the Great Barrier Reef. Print some of the photos (you can ask your teacher for help) and use them to make a poster of the Great Barrier Reef. Use your notes too.

Materials: computer with Internet access, dictionary, printer, paper, poster, scissors, glue, markers

NOTES

Where	
What	
Size	
1st Explorer	
Damaged by	1.
	2.
	3.
	4.

ANSWER KEY

1C

■ Fill in the missing articles.

the – ✘ – ✘ – the – The – the – ✘ – the – the – ✘ – the – ✘ – ✘ – the

2A

■ Find a separate title for each paragraph.

Example:

Australia's first inhabitants – First Europeans in Australia – Captain Cook discovers Australia – New animals discovered – Australia claimed for England – Aborigines do not celebrate Australia Day

2B

■ Fill in the table.

discover – discoverer – discovery
settle – settler – settlement
imprison – prisoner – imprisonment
travel – traveller – travel
find – finder – finding
found – founder – foundation
originate – originator – origin
historian – history

2D

■ Translate the text.

Ned Kelly's letzte Schlacht in Glenrowan

(A) Ned Kelly ist Australiens Robin Hood. Er war bei den Armen beliebt und wurde von der Polizei bekämpft. Er führte ein kriminelles Leben. Er überfiel Banken und stahl Vieh von reichen Bauern. Er war ein extrem guter Reiter, und zusammen mit seiner Bande gewann er oft Schlachten gegen die Polizei. Er war durch einen Helm und eine Rüstung geschützt, die er selbst gemacht hatte.

(B) Hier in Glenrowan kämpfte er seine letzte Schlacht, die bis in die Nacht dauerte. An diesem Tag kämpfte er gegen eine große Zahl Polizisten. Er war erst geschlagen, als die Polizisten merkten, dass seine Beine ungeschützt waren, und ihm in die Beine schossen. Er war erst 25 Jahre alt, als man ihn endlich fing. Er wurde am 11. November 1880 in Melbourne gehängt.

2E

■ Fill in the missing keywords.

Examples:

coast, beach – explorer, tourist, holidaymaker – marsupial, animal – sports, water sports – Aborigines, explorers, Australian history – plant, eucalyptus tree

3B

■ Unscramble the words.

1 reporter, 2 interview, 3 headline, 4 foreign correspondent, 5 broadcast, 6 weather forecast, 7 article

3C

■ Fill in the missing words.

years – radios – everybody's – sports – day's – school's – schools

4B

■ Match each expression with the correct explanation.

A 7, B 8, C 10, D 5, E 12, F 6, G 9, H 2, I 3, J 1, K 11, L 4

4C

■ Fill in the right words.

much/any – no – any – some/a lot of – some/a lot of – some/a lot of – a lot of/some – much – some

4D

■ Try to have a conversation.

Example:

Yes, of course. Shall I explain the warning signs to you?
You may only swim between the red and yellow flags.
You mustn't go in the water if there is a red flag.
You must be careful because there are high waves here and strong currents.

You must watch out for dangerous jellyfish.
You mustn't jump into the water.
It's a pleasure! Have fun on the beach!

4E

■ Write down the meanings of the words.
Billabong: A water hole
Billy: A tin can for boiling water used by campers
Coolibah Tree: A kind of eucalyptus tree
Jumbuck: A sheep
Squatter: A person who has taken claim on a piece of land
Swag: A bundle of personal belongings
Swagman: A tramp; a man carrying a swag, walking on foot, doing occasional jobs here and there or begging for money
Trooper: A cavalry soldier. Like the squatter, he rides on a horse (= thoroughbred)
Tucker-bag: A bag to keep tucker (= food) in
Waltzing Matilda: Tramping through the country with a swag on one's back.
The song is about a tramp who has caught a sheep. He is surprised by a soldier and a squatter, and jumps into the water hole to escape them.

5B

■ Try to find the words.
1. parasol/sun umbrella
2. compass
3. map
4. water canister
5. tools
6. offroad vehicle
7. provisions, food supply
8. first aid kit
9. radio, HF-radio

5C

■ Put the sentences in the right order.
AYERS ROCK
■ Change the sentences to reported speech.
Example:
He said that he had rescued a family; there had been four people: two parents and a boy and a girl. He had found them next to their car. The family had been suffering because they hadn't prepared their journey very well. He added that it was lucky that they had brought a lot of water but they had forgotten to bring a radio. They had tried to use their mobile phones to call for help but it hadn't worked. They had had to wait five days until someone had found them. Their water supply had been used up, and the children had been very weak. He said that he and his partner got to them just in time. They were fine now. He concluded that it was important to always carry a radio in the outback.

6C

■ Fill in the table.
poisonous – more poisonous – the most poisonous; long – longer – the longest; aggressive – more aggressive – the most aggressive; big – bigger – the biggest; speedy – speedier – the speediest

6D

■ Try to write the story.
Example:
One Sunday afternoon Mr and Mrs Jones were at home in their living-room, wondering what they could do. Mrs Jones wanted to knit a pair of socks, and Mr Jones still hadn't read his newspaper. He fetched the paper and wanted to sit down in his favourite armchair, but the cat was fast asleep in it. Mr Jones gave it a pat, but it wouldn't go away. Angrily, he chased it away with the newspaper and sat down.
He found an article on the most poisonous animals in Australia and started to read. Mrs Jones felt sorry for the cat. She put her knitting needles down and played with the cat. The cat loved playing with balls of wool.

It was chasing one and turned round and round.
Soon it got so entangled in the wool that it couldn't free itself anymore. Mrs Jones laughed. She went to get some scissors and cut the poor cat loose. Mr Jones didn't notice anything – he just carried on reading his newspaper.
Suddenly Mr Jones got up and climbed up the bookcase. He was so terrified that he was shaking! He pointed at a black creature on the floor. "Help!" he cried and refused to come down.
Mrs Jones investigated the situation quickly: She was just going to pick up the black creature, when Mr Jones shouted: "Stop! Don't touch it! It might be Australia's most poisonous spider! It has enough poison to kill 60 grown men! You could die! We don't have any antidote in the house!"
Mrs Jones laughed and explained: "But darling! This is only wool! It is not poisonous!" Mr Jones was very relieved and climbed down again. He was embarrassed and wanted to sit down so he could hide behind his newspaper. But who was sitting on his armchair, looking triumphant? The cat!

6E

■ Take notes.
Where: North-eastern Australia, off the coast of Queensland in the Coral Sea
What: The world's largest coral reef, many colonies of corals
Size: Over 2000 km in length
1st Explorer: James Cook, 1770
Damaged by: 1. Global warming (coral bleaching, tropical storms), 2. Sugar industry, 3. Crown-of-Thorns starfish, 4. Visitors (tourists).